Native American
Religions

ROB STAEGER

Senior Consulting Editor Dr. Troy Johnson
Professor of History and American Indian Studies
California State University

MASON CREST PUBLISHERS • PHILADELPHIA

NATIVE AMERICAN LIFE

Native American
Religions

ROB STAEGER

Senior Consulting Editor Dr. Troy Johnson
Professor of History and American Indian Studies
California State University

MASON CREST PUBLISHERS • PHILADELPHIA

NATIVE AMERICAN LIFE

This book is dedicated to my sister Sally, who sees the divine in everyone much more clearly than I.

Mason Crest Publishers
370 Reed Road
Broomall PA 19008
www.masoncrest.com

First printing

1 3 5 7 9 8 6 4 2

Library of Congress Cataloging-in-Publication Data
on file at the Library of Congress

ISBN 1-59084-122-0

Frontispiece: Birds of prey circle a heap of human and buffalo skulls
left as a shrine or offering on the prairie by the Mandan Indians.

Table of Contents

Introduction

For hundreds of years the dominant image of the Native American has been that of a stoic warrior, often wearing a full-length eagle feather headdress, riding a horse in pursuit of the buffalo, or perhaps surrounding some unfortunate wagon train filled with innocent west-bound American settlers. Unfortunately there has been little written or made available to the general public to dispel this erroneous generalization. This misrepresentation has resulted in an image of native people that has been translated into books, movies, and television programs that have done little to look deeply into the native worldview, cosmology, and daily life. Not until the 1990 movie *Dances with Wolves* were native people portrayed as having a human persona. For the first time, native people could express humor, sorrow, love, hate, peace, and warfare. For the first time native people could express themselves in words other than "ugh" or "Yes, Kemo Sabe." This series has been written to provide a more accurate and encompassing journey into the world of the Native Americans.

When studying the native world of the Americas, it is extremely important to understand that there are few "universals" that apply across tribal boundaries. With over 500 nations and 300 language groups the worlds of the Native Americans were diverse. The traditions of one group may or may not have been shared by neighboring groups. Sports, games, dance, subsistence patterns, clothing, and religion differed—greatly in some instances. And although nearly all native groups observed festivals and ceremonies necessary to insure the renewal of their worlds, these too varied greatly.

Of equal importance to the breaking down of old myopic and stereotypic images is that the authors in this series credit Native

Americans with a sense of agency. Contrary to the views held by the Europeans who came to North and South America and established the United States, Canada, Mexico, and other nations, some Native American tribes had sophisticated political and governing structures—that of the member nations of the Iroquois League, for example. Europeans at first denied that native people had religions but rather "worshiped the devil," and demanded that Native Americans abandon their religions for the Christian worldview. The readers of this series will learn that native people had well-established religions, led by both men and women, long before the European invasion began in the 16th and 17th centuries.

Gender roles also come under scrutiny in this series. European settlers in the northeastern area of the present-day United States found it appalling that native women were "treated as drudges" and forced to do the men's work in the agricultural fields. They failed to understand, as the reader will see, that among this group the women owned the fields and scheduled the harvests. Europeans also failed to understand that Iroquois men were diplomats and controlled over one million square miles of fur-trapping area. While Iroquois men sat at the governing council, Iroquois clan matrons caucused with tribal members and told the men how to vote.

These are small examples of the material contained in this important series. The reader is encouraged to use the extended bibliographies provided with each book to expand his or her area of specific interest.

Dr. Troy Johnson
Professor of History and American Indian Studies
California State University

1 Religion without Words

There are more than 250 different Native American languages. Each one describes life in great detail, yet not one has a word for "religion." This doesn't mean that spirituality was unimportant to the Native Americans, however. In fact, the opposite is true. Native American spiritual life was so rich that it could not be boxed in with one word. Religion touched everything in life, and they felt no need to keep it separate. Everything was religion—a separate word was unnecessary.

Native Americans have no sacred book, like the Bible or the Koran. Some tribes kept records through symbols on wooden sticks or *wampum* belts. Traditions were primarily passed down through storytelling.

Native American religions differ throughout the Americas. In Central and South America, the natives built elaborate temples, such as the one pictured here, for worship. The Indians of the American southwest created buildings called kivas, which were used for religious purposes. Other tribes of North America had sacred areas that they visited to worship.

A Native American storyteller captivates his audience in this 19th-century illustration. Because most Native American tribes did not have written languages, the rituals and prayers used for religious ceremonies were passed down orally from generation to generation.

Native stories begin in different ways. The Pima and Papago begin a story by saying, "They say it happened long ago…." Zuñi stories begin with a conversation. The storyteller says, "Now we are taking it up." The audience responds, "Yes, indeed." Then the storyteller says, "Now it begins to be made," and begins the story. By telling the story, the storyteller is making the events happen again; it becomes true once more.

In general, Native Americans believed that there was a divine spirit that ran through all things. Different tribes had different names for it. The Algonquian tribes called this spirit Manitou, while the Iroquois called it Orenda. To the Inuit, it was Sila. On the Great Plains, it was Wakanda. The Maya of South America called it K'ul.

The basic Native American belief is known as *animism*. Animism is a belief system that gives divine qualities to animals and objects. To the Indians, any coyote might be the trickster god Coyote. Corn was Corn Mother, and the river was Long Man.

This animism leads to a respect for nature and all aspects of it. People had to live in harmony with nature, in order to treat the divine spirit with respect. Native American legends stress that men and animals are equals.

Since the spirit world was apparent in nature, Native Americans felt close ties to it. Their relationship with the spirit world was immediate and practical. Religion wasn't a mental or emotional state of mind. Wakanda was all around, all the time. If you asked the gods for rain, rain would come. If it didn't, you could ask again, paying closer attention to how you asked. A proper ritual could force the gods into granting a request. One mistake, however, and the gods might not answer your prayers. Sometimes, spirits were stubborn. If they didn't do what you asked, there were rituals to scold or punish them.

11

NATIVE AMERICAN LIFE

This painting was found on the wall of a kiva in New Mexico. Kivas were circular structures that were used for religious ceremonies. Tribal meetings were also held there.

The spirit world affected everybody, not just priests and *shamans*. People had dreams and visions, which were viewed as messages from the gods. Special rituals, such as the vision quest and the sweat lodge ceremony, helped people contact spirits.

Everyone dealt with the spirit world on one level or another. After all, the spirits had a hand in everything people did. From birth to death, while hunting or eating or playing games, the spirit world was present. Regardless of the name, the spirits were felt from the woodlands of the northeast to the Andes Mountains in South America. Tribes had many differences, but their beliefs include many common threads. §

Manetto Indianorum,

The Lenape and Delaware tribes of northeastern North America believed in a spirit, called Manitou, which was part of all living things. This 18th-century woodcut shows a carving that appeared over the doorway of a Lenape home. It is believed to represent the Great Horned Serpent, an evil spirit of the Lenape religion.

2 Religions of the Northeast

The northeastern United States and eastern Canada were home to the woodland Indians. These included the Algonquian, the Shawnee, the Cree, and the tribes of the Iroquois Confederacy. The people of these tribes believed in a spirit called Manitou.

Early white missionaries equated Manitou with the Christian idea of God. However, this was not exactly accurate. The concepts were similar, but there was an important difference. To a Christian, God created everything. Algonquians believed that Manitou *was* everything in the world. Trees, a raccoon, the moon—all were Manitou. No one entity created everything.

At one point, a French missionary met with some Fox Indians in Wisconsin, who welcomed him. The missionary had heard of Manitou and thought he could use it to *convert* the Indians to Christianity. He said that Jesus was a powerful Manitou. The Fox warriors tested this idea. They painted crosses on their bodies before a battle with the

The name "medicine man" came from French trappers. They noticed that shamans were often called upon to heal the sick, so they called them *medecins*, meaning doctors.

Sioux. They won, and praised Jesus Manitou. The next year, they fought the Sioux again. This time, they lost badly. They returned to the village and tore down the crosses. After some time, the French priest returned, but he was not allowed into the village.

Tobacco was important to the Native Americans. Almost every North American tribe used it in religious ceremonies. The first puffs of smoke were always offered to the Great Spirit. Worship often began with puffs from a long pipe called a calumet. Calumets were usually made of a red stone called catlinite. The Great Lakes Indians were sometimes called the Calumet People because they valued tobacco so much.

People also reached out to the Great Spirit through **vision quests**. Going on a vision quest was one of the necessary steps to becoming an adult. A young man beginning a vision quest left his village and isolated himself for several days. During this time, he **fasted** and prayed for a vision.

Eventually, the person on the vision quest would receive a message or vision from an animal. This animal would be his spirit animal. It would advise and guard him for the rest of his life. From then on, he

Catlinite was named after George Catlin, a well-known white painter of Native Americans during the first half of the 19th century. It comes from Pipestone, Minnesota, which is now a national monument. It is illegal for anyone but Native Americans to mine catlinite.

This drawing by Karl Bodmer shows a long pipe, or calumet. The Native Americans used calumets in many religious and social ceremonies. Because the pipes were sometimes smoked after agreements were concluded with white settlers, calumets have been called "peace pipes."

17

would pay extra attention to that animal. Whether seen in a dream or in waking life, a spirit animal was always considered a sign. Some people gained special powers from their vision quests. The powers could be skill at hunting or healing powers. People rarely spoke about their vision quests—they were considered sacred and private.

Dreams, on the other hand, often held meaning for the entire community. Native Americans did not consider dreaming separate from everyday life. Instead, dreams were viewed as important messages from the spirit world. The people of the Iroquois Nation took dreams especially seriously. They held a festival called the Ceremony of the Great Riddle. One by one, men, women, and children would relate

their dreams. Experts in the tribe would explain what the dreams meant. Some people would talk about old dreams. They would say what had happened when they followed the dream's signs.

The Ojibwa also took dreams seriously. They believed that a person's good traits were given to him during dreams. They sang special "dream songs" and wore charms to get powerful dreams.

Unlike Christians, woodland Indians did not have priests. Instead, they had shamans. Shamans had an important role in the tribe. They cured the sick and spoke with the gods. A shaman did not study for his spiritual authority—at least, not at first. It came to him in a dream or vision. Shamans were also called medicine men, although there were some female shamans.

Different tribes had different medicine societies with different rules and traditions. The Iroquois False Face Society would dance and chant wearing masks to drive illnesses away. The masks had specific characters, such as Spoon Nose or Crooked Face.

19

The Ojibwa had the Grand Medicine Society. Both men and women could join, although it was expensive. Students gave valuable goods to join and advance in the Medicine Society. There were four levels to

Members of the Iroquois False Face Society wore wooden masks like this one while performing religious or healing rituals. In spring and fall they went from house to house, shaking turtle-shell rattles and chanting to drive away the evil spirits that caused sickness.

NATIVE AMERICAN LIFE

the program. Members learned new prayers and rituals with each step. Each level took a long time to learn and required great dedication. Only rarely did someone complete the fourth level.

European settlement changed Native American religions in different ways. In the northeast, the most effective missionaries were the Quakers. This was a branch of Christianity that preached nonviolence and followed a strict moral code. However, even they were not immediately effective. Most woodland Indians kept their own religion. This was partially due to a teacher known as the Delaware Prophet. In

AN ALGONQUIAN LEGEND

When the world was young, the god Michabo was hunting. His wolves found some dogs and chased them into an enormous lake. Michabo waded in after them, and the lake overflowed. Its water covered the entire earth.

Michabo wanted to rebuild the land, but he needed a piece of earth to begin. He asked the raven, who flew around, but couldn't find any. Then he asked the otter. He also came up empty. Finally, he asked the muskrat. She found him a small piece of earth. From it, Michabo re-created dry land.

When he was finished, he saw that the trees had no branches. The flooding had washed them away. He shot his arrows into the trees, and they became branches. Then Michabo married the muskrat woman. Their children became the human race.

the 1760s, he taught the Indians to free themselves by uniting, avoiding alcohol and guns, and praying only to the Great Spirit. Pontiac, an Ottawa chief, supported him. The prophet's message proved popular, and the people united under Pontiac. In 1763, Pontiac declared war on the British settlers and captured eight forts. Pontiac's War ended in 1766, when he signed a peace treaty with the British.

In 1799, a Seneca chief named Handsome Lake began to have visions. He started preaching what he had learned as the Gaiwiio, or "good word." It was a reaction to the problems caused by the fact that men's traditional role was changing. Tribes had nowhere left to hunt, and they depended more on farming. This made the men restless.

Handsome Lake's teachings set down a moral code combining Catholicism, Quaker values, and Iroquois traditions. Drunkenness was outlawed. So were gambling, wife beating, and witchcraft. The Gaiwiio also renewed traditional rituals, such as the Strawberry Ceremony and the Midwinter Ceremony. When Handsome Lake died, his nephew organized his teachings into the Handsome Lake Church. Many Iroquois still practice his teachings. ⑤

21

NATIVE AMERICAN LIFE

This painting by George Catlin shows
the interior of a Native American sweat
lodge during a ceremony. The sweat
lodge was used by the Indians to cleanse
both their bodies and their souls.

3 Religions of the Southeast

No one knows what the earliest inhabitants of the southeast called themselves. However, *archaeologists* call them the Mississippians. The culture sprang up around the Mississippi River and spread east and west. Mississippians worshiped the sun and built temples out of mounds of earth. They had a complex farming society led by a chief known as the Great Sun. Every morning, he would face the east and greet his brother, the rising sun. He would draw a line in the sky from east to west. This told the sun how to travel in the sky.

By the time Europeans arrived in North America, most Mississippian tribes had disappeared. The only one that remained was the Natchez; the rest of the area was occupied by tribes that had settled the area later. They were the Choctaw, Chickasaw, Cherokee, Creek, and Timucua peoples.

Descended from the Mississippians, the Natchez differed from other tribes, as was shown in their reaction to death. Many tribes would remove all traces of someone who died. Graves were never marked. Often, people would not even say a dead man's name. Keeping his things around might give his ghost a reason to stay by them. Even if the spirit was a friend in life, getting haunted by a ghost only meant trouble.

Sometimes, the person's horse or dog would be killed to serve him in the afterlife. The Natchez took this even further. If a powerful chief died, his slaves and relatives volunteered to be strangled. It was felt that the chief deserved a large group around him in the hereafter.

The Natchez died out in the early 1700s, weakened by constant warfare with neighboring tribes and the arrival of French settlers. The other tribes settled into a peaceful, lawful routine. They became known as the Five Civilized Tribes. The tribes had their own rituals and beliefs, which separated them from both the Natchez and the whites. Instead of centering their religion on the sun, they focused on the wind. Their name for the creator of the world was Master of Breath.

They divided the world into three regions. The upper world was where gods and spirits lived. The middle world included humans and animals. The lower world was home to strange creatures and spirits.

The gods and spirits of the upper world were invisible. They didn't affect everyday life unless called forth by a ritual. The lower world had other spirits, called the little people. They were tiny, mischievous imps. They liked children, but it was bad luck for adults to see one.

There were two types of religious figures in the southeastern tribes. As in the northeast, there were shamans, whose powers came to them through visions. Here, however, there were also priests. Priests studied for their religious authority. They learned the tribal lore and the proper rituals. Unlike shamans, there were no women priests. Priests were those whom people chose to speak to the gods. Shamans were those whom the gods chose to speak with the people.

Shamans and priests contacted the spirit world through rituals. Some rituals called for a foul black drink made from twigs and yaupon holly. It was difficult to swallow. Most people threw up immediately.

Yaupon holly is one of the few native plants in North America that contains caffeine. Caffeine is a *diuretic*; it helps people to sweat. According to Timucua belief, this sweating allowed the drinker to remove physical and spiritual impurities from his system. Only adult men could drink the black drink. These men sipped it at the morning gatherings while they discussed tribal matters.

However, there were other uses of the black drink. If you drink several cups of any hot liquid, especially a caffeinated hot liquid, you are going to get sick. The Timucuas used this as an extreme form of purification. If the men were going on an important hunt or to battle, they needed a lot of luck, which required them to be ritually pure. The men gulped down the black drink and then vomited profusely or struggled to hold it down. After that, they were so hyper from the caffeine that they often succeeded in their endeavors.

Another method of purification was a sweat lodge ceremony. Sweat lodges were used throughout North America. A sweat lodge is a special hut with heated stones in the center. Water is poured on the stones, creating steam. The heat is tremendous—men would almost pass out from it. They often reported great visions. Afterward, the men would rush from the lodge and jump into a nearby stream or roll in the snow.

> **Even in a sweat lodge, running water was important to the Cherokee. The water they poured over the rocks was always taken from a waterfall.**

The most important event of the southeastern Indians' year was the Green Corn Festival. It ended with a ritual called Busk, which took place when the corn ripened in July or August. It was designed to give thanks to the Great Corn Mother and Sun Father. Corn could not be eaten before Busk.

Busk began with men sprinkling sand in the town square. There, they would pray, fast, and drink the black drink. The women and children of the town cleaned their homes from top to bottom. Every fire in the village was put out.

In the center of town, a new sacred fire would be lit. People lit *tinder* from the central fire and used the flame to start a new fire in their homes. The new fires represented a new start. Like modern New Year's celebrations, Busk was a time for making resolutions. Also, it was

The American artist George Catlin made this drawing of Native Americans performing the Green Corn Ceremony. This summer ritual was the most sacred time of the year for many tribes of the southeast.

27

a time for forgiveness. Sins confessed in the town square were forgiven. Busk ended with a big feast of corn. People gambled, danced, and played sports to celebrate.

As mentioned previously, Native Americans held animals in high esteem. Animals were powerful creatures, not to be taken lightly. The Creeks, for instance, believed that each animal was related to an illness. The animal could cause or cure the disease. For example, in the weeks before a *lacrosse* game, players would not touch a frog. They believed that contact with the frog would make their bones as brittle as a frog's.

During the presidential administration of Andrew Jackson (inset), the U.S. government forced many of the Native Americans living in the southeast to leave their lands. The forced march of the Cherokee to Oklahoma during the 1830s has become known as the Trail of Tears.

Many tribes in the southeast *revered* bears. Creeks and Cherokee believed bears sacrificed themselves so that people could eat. After a bear hunt, villages would thank the bears who died. They would lay clothes out for the spirit of the bear, welcoming it to the feast. They would put out bowls of nuts, berries, and honey—things bears liked to eat.

Native Americans had strong beliefs about the entire natural world. An example of this is the Cherokee's relationship to the river. The river was the center of Cherokee spirituality. It was called Long Man, a giant with his head in the mountains and his feet in the lowlands. The rippling of the river was Long Man murmuring. Purification in a stream or river was important to the Cherokee. Their **longhouse** was almost always located near running water.

Most rituals happened at the river. When a baby was born, the mother and a priest would take it to the river. The priest would hold the baby and bend down to the river seven times, saying prayers. Then he would take some river water and sprinkle it on the baby.

If someone were having bad dreams, she would also go to the water with a priest. Bad dreams were expected to come true if a priest didn't stop them. They were signs of a curse. There was only one thing to do with bad dreams. Since they would always come true regardless of where they were, the priest sent them somewhere else. The dreamer waded into the water, wearing only a shirt. The priest would pray and ask where she wanted the dreams to go. The dreamer would name somewhere far away. The priest would then ask the beaver to carry the dreams away.

When the Europeans arrived, the people of the Five Civilized Tribes tried to adapt to white customs, but it was no use. In 1830, the United States government passed the Indian Removal Act. Southeastern Indians were driven into Oklahoma. The march was devastating, causing many deaths. It became known as the Trail of Tears. In moving the tribes, the U.S. government denied them the land where their religion was rooted. S

29

NATIVE AMERICAN LIFE

This 1907 photograph shows three leaders of the Chilkat tribe, which lived in the northwestern United States and Canada. The men are holding ceremonial rattles and wearing blankets woven from dyed cedar bark decorated with tribal symbols. The man in the middle is wearing a special totem headdress. These ornate clothes were worn during potlatch ceremonies, during which members of northwestern tribes threw large parties and gave valuable gifts to their guests.

Religions of the Northwest and Far North

The northwest coast was home to many tribes. They were some of the richest people in native America. Fish and game were all around. Everything people needed was at their fingertips. People often held competitions, called **potlatches**, in which they gave each other lavish gifts. This served two purposes. First, it showed a family's wealth. Second, a person given a gift at a potlatch was obligated to pay it back, but with a gift of greater value. Anything less meant a loss of face. This led to neighbors bankrupting each other to keep the respect of their communities.

The potlatches often included performances by shamans and dance societies. In the Nootka and Kwakiutl tribes, the performances began before the potlatch even started. First, members of the dance society, dressed as supernatural beings, carried off a villager. The captive would stay out of sight until the potlatch. He would then explain that he had been kidnapped but had gained supernatural powers and escaped. He would perform magic tricks to demonstrate his powers.

As in other regions, animals were central to the northwestern native worldview and history. The Eastern Shoshones believed that Wolf created the solar system and the people. They call Wolf Pia Apo, or Big

Father. The trickster Coyote came to the land before people. He chased most of the evil out of the area. He is known as Tei Apo—Little Father.

Further north, Inuit people believed that Raven created the world. Raven was considered a clever, mischievous god. The world he made was a flat plate on four wooden pillars. Thus, it was important to be careful during a hunt. Careless hunters could fall off the sides of the plate.

The people of the far north didn't have time for elaborate religious ceremonies. Food was scarce, and they were constantly hunting. They also believed that animals allowed themselves to be killed to help people survive in the harsh land. Like other Indians, the Inuit believed in the Great Spirit that ran through everything. Their name for it is Sila. Sila could be found in storms and in sunlight and in every animal and plant. The Inuit believed Sila was everywhere.

The Inuit may not have had elaborate ceremonies, but there were some areas that were considered particularly sacred. These included caves, cliffs, and high rocks. Men seeking power and visions would go to these places, bringing offerings of animal skins or feathers.

Unlike most Native Americans, tribes of the far north believed in *reincarnation*. This is the belief that a dead person's soul returns to earth in a new body. If a Tanana hunter could not kill a certain animal, it was because the animal had a human spirit, the tribe believed.

Since there was little farming, hunting was extremely important to northern tribes. In addition to curing disease, shamans made predictions about the hunt. A shaman would burn an arrow and rub its ashes on a moose bone. Then he would put the bone in the fire. If the

This Sioux picture writing was done on the skin of a bison. It shows the Sun Dance, a religious festival that tested the endurance of the tribe's warriors. The purpose of the ritual was to thank the spirit of the Sun for past favors, and to ask the Sun to protect the tribe. In some cases warriors performed the ritual for purification before going into battle. In this drawing, the cross at the center of the circle indicates the presence of a white man at the ceremony.

shaman smelled burning meat, the hunt would go well.

Despite the importance of hunting, some animals were off-limits. The Slave tribe did not kill wolves, and the Dog Rib Indians would not eat weasels. Spiritual *taboos* also prevented many tribes from hunting certain animals.

The spiritual connection to nature prompted Native Americans to give something back to the earth. Often, they sacrificed food or

A HAIDA LEGEND

Long ago, there was a great fish shortage. A mother gave her child the last piece of salmon. It was old, but still good to eat. The boy ate a small piece and pushed the rest away. The Salmon King heard of this and got angry.

The Salmon People kidnapped the boy. They let him swim with their children and called him Salmon Boy. He was there for a year. One day, the Salmon King told him that he could eat one of the salmon as long as he put all the parts that were not good to eat back in the ocean. Salmon Boy did this, but kept one eye. Later, he noticed that a salmon was crying. The salmon uncovered his face. He was missing an eye. Salmon Boy saw this and let go of the eye he was holding. It reappeared in the crying salmon's face.

One day, Salmon Boy swam to shore. His mother caught him in a net. Salmon Boy stayed with her and grew to be a great shaman. He told people they must always put their fish bones back in the water to show respect for the salmon.

tobacco. People were rarely harmed in a sacrifice, but there were exceptions. Every year, the Pawnee would capture and sacrifice a young girl as part of their spring rite to bring fertility to their crops.

After a purification ritual, warriors would raid an enemy camp. There, they would kidnap a 13-year-old girl. In the Pawnee camp, the girl would be treated like a princess. She ate the best food and wore fine clothes. Meanwhile, men would build a *scaffold*.

On the appointed day, just before dawn, the kidnapped girl would be taken to the scaffold. Her left side was painted black, for the night. Her right side would be red, for the morning star. The Pawnee would tie her to the scaffold and place buffalo meat below her. They would smoke tobacco and wait for the morning star to rise. When it did, a warrior would shoot an arrow through the girl's heart. The men would then take her body east and lay it on the ground. They would sing about how her body would nourish the earth. When the men returned to the lodge, people would sing and dance, rejoicing at the girl's sacrifice.

In 1816, a young Pawnee warrior named Man Chief changed this. He thought that whites would attack if they saw the sacrifice. Therefore, Man Chief rode to the scaffold before the girl was killed. He untied her and told her to ride his horse back to her own people. This was risky. He might have been killed. Instead, he was regarded with awe and disbelief by his people. Legend said that to touch the maiden before the sacrifice meant death. Instead, Man Chief survived. He became a great Pawnee leader. With few exceptions, the sacrifices ended after this event.

35

NATIVE AMERICAN LIFE

By the late 1880s, U.S. soldiers had forced the
Sioux and other native tribes onto reservations
and destroyed their way of life. In 1889, a Sioux
name Wovoka had a vision: the buffalo herds
would return and the whites would leave if the
people of the Great Plains performed the Ghost
Dance. This ritual soon spread among the tribes
of the Great Plains. Unfortunately, many whites
became nervous because of the dancing. Their
attempt to stop the Ghost Dance ritual led to the
tragic massacre of several hundred Sioux men,
women, and children at Wounded Knee Creek in
December 1890.

Other cultural shifts were sparked by concern about the whites. The Ghost Dance religion began in the northwest during the late 1800s. The tribes had lost much of their territory to whites during this time. Native peoples looked to religion to change this. The Ghost Dance sought to reestablish the older traditions and form a bond between the living and their dead ancestors. It was an attempt to recreate the past. It emphasized personal responsibility and the practice of traditions in daily life.

Eventually, the Ghost Dance religion spread to the Great Plains. The Lakota, in particular, eagerly embraced this belief. The dance itself alarmed white onlookers. They believed it was a preparation for war. Dancers wore shirts painted with symbols. The believed that white men's bullets could not pierce the shirts. Many Plains tribes combined the dance with the more vigorous Sun Dance. The result, although intended to be peaceful, was quite fierce to behold. In December 1890, the Seventh Cavalry was sent to keep order. At Wounded Knee, they massacred 200 Sioux men, women, and children from Big Foot's band of Lakota. The slaughter contributed to the religion's decline.

In the far north, traditions changed little, even after the United States bought Alaska from Russia in 1867. Inuit customs were practiced side-by-side with the Russian Orthodox faith. The Russians had begun missionary work in 1824, and many people celebrated both traditions. The area became more settled in the middle of the 20th century. Only then did further cultural shifts take place. ⑤

37

NATIVE AMERICAN LIFE

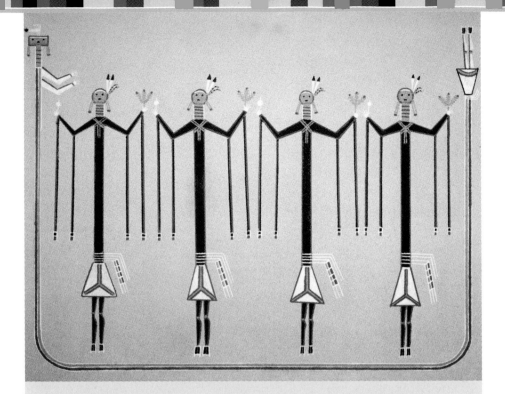

This Navajo sand painting was intended to ensure a good harvest. The Navajo and other tribes of the southwest used sand paintings as part of their religious ceremonies, as well as for healing rituals. Holy men of the tribe would make a round bed of sand—sometimes as large as 20 feet in diameter—and then decorate it with various designs and symbols. Color was added to the painting by using ground up charcoal, root bark, crushed flowers, and pollen. The maker of the sand painting always included a deliberate mistake, however, because the Navajo believed only the Great Spirit could create something that was completely perfect.

5 Religions of the Southwest

The Mongollon were among the first people to live in the southwest. They made excellent pottery, which was often buried with its maker. Before an artist was buried, his pottery would be punctured. The hole released the part of the artist's spirit inside it.

The Mongollons were the ancestors of the Yuma and Mohave Indians. Like the Iroquois of the northeast, the Mohave also built their worldview around dreams. They have a concept called "The Great Dream." The Great Dream is a dream every person dreams before they are born. Like all dreams, it has a message. It tells people how to live their lives. People forget this dream during infancy and childhood. The Mohave try to remember this dream, however, through visions and rituals. Some people are successful and guide their lives by this dream.

Both Navajos and Apaches held four-day rituals to celebrate children becoming adults. The Navajo ceremony was called Kinalda. Children would grind corn, run foot races, and dance with adults. The adults wore masks representing the gods. Before the dance ended, the children would also put on masks. From then on, they related to the spirit world as adults. The fourth night would be a long feast with dancing and singing.

Pueblo Indians worshipped in kivas. Kivas were circular structures dug out of the earth. While there was often some part of the kiva above ground, most of it was underground. This kept the area cool, which was important in the hot climate. Four pillars held up the roof. Inside were benches, storage areas, and pits for building fires. Light streamed in from several open areas. Kivas were used for religious ceremonies and as meeting halls. Generally, only men could enter kivas. Women could enter only for special rituals.

In July, the Hopi would hold their Niman ceremony. Niman translates roughly to "home dance." The Hopi believed that supernatural beings called kachinas served as messengers between gods and humans. Kachinas lived with the Hopi through the winter and spring. They returned to their mountain home in the summer. Niman celebrated the kachinas' return to the mountains.

Men often belonged to kachina societies. To celebrate Niman, society members dressed as kachinas. The dressing ceremony was held in secret in a kiva. Men could see it, as could women who had just married. Eventually, the kachinas would come out from the kiva and dance.

Children were told that the dancing men really were kachinas. As the dance ended, women threw blankets over the children. Then the dancers returned to the kiva. Once they were out of sight, the blankets

Kachina societies performed healing rituals, much like eastern medicine societies. Women could only join a kachina society if they had been cured by one of their rituals.

The eyes of this Hopi kachina doll represent rain clouds, while the lashes are rain. Hopi children believe the dolls contain spirits. Young members of the Hopi tribe are initiated into kachina societies when they are around eight years old.

would come off. People would point to the sky and watch the kachinas flying away. Children were encouraged to believe in the kachinas, just as children today believe in Santa Claus. When they grew older, they were told about the kachina societies.

Dancing was important to the Indians of the west. One of the most sacred ceremonies of the western plains was the Sun Dance. Near the summer *solstice*, someone would dream of the ceremony. People would begin fasting and going to the sweat lodge to prepare. The first day of the Sun Dance was spent building the sun pole and the sun lodge. Dancers circled around the pole, praying and singing.

Sometimes, the Sun Dance included an *okipa*. This was a grueling, painful trial. Men volunteered for it because it sometimes

AN ARIKARA LEGEND

Long ago, buffalo stood on two feet and walked like people. They were more dangerous then, and killed and ate humans. One day, a buffalo woman taught a man named Cut-nose how to fight the buffalo. Cut-nose shot a buffalo with a special arrow, and the wounded buffalo began walking on four legs. Seeing this, the other buffalo grabbed the human flesh they were eating. They stuffed it under their armpits and ran. Cut-nose and other humans shot them with the special arrows. When the buffalo were hit, the meat they carried changed with them. Thus, the Arikara do not eat the part of the buffalo under the foreleg out of respect for their human ancestors.

The Sun Dance, as practiced by the tribes of the plains, was a brutal ceremony. Young warriors were not allowed to eat for several days. Then, shallow cuts were made in the skin over the warrior's chest and a sharpened stick was pushed through the skin. Ropes were then attached to the sticks, and the young man was expected to hang suspended until the sticks tore through his flesh and released him.

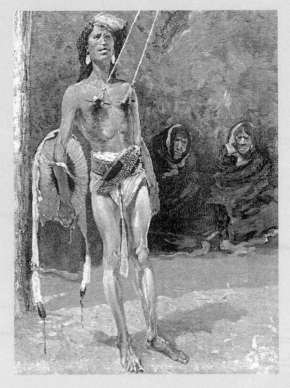

The warriors then sang and danced in a circle, each hoping to receive a vision. This Frederic Remington drawing of a Blackfoot Indian participating in the Sun Dance was published in *Harper's Weekly* in 1890.

produced visions. The ritual began with buffalo warriors "capturing" and torturing the participants. They thrust wooden skewers through the participant's back and chest muscles. Then, they would be lifted onto leather straps. Participants would hang by the skewers from the lodge ceiling or the sun pole itself. The warriors dangled backward, facing the sun with their eyes open.

Lakota Sioux spiritual leaders take part in a peyote ritual on the Rosebud reservation in South Dakota. The peyote cactus contains a drug called mescaline, which causes hallucinogenic sensations when eaten. Members of the Native American Church are the only people permitted to eat peyote buttons, and use is restricted to church ceremonies.

Despite the tremendous pain, they were not allowed to cry out. Around them, their relatives and neighbors sang and drummed. Eventually, the warriors called for their possessions. Their families handed them armor and other items. Eventually, the weight of the items caused their muscles to tear, and they dropped off the skewers. The U.S. government tried to ban the Sun Dance because of the brutality of the okipa.

In 1890, John Wilson began the Big Moon Society. The society's ceremonies included peyote rituals. Peyote is a small cactus that grows in Mexico and New Mexico. It produces small buttons, which are **hallucinogens**. The peyote was treated like an animal—it was hunted, not harvested. It was important to shoot the plant with an arrow before taking the buttons. People who ate peyote often saw visions. Wilson intended the cult to reestablish Native American values. When he died, the cult began to embrace many aspects of Christianity. However, peyote rituals are still practiced today as part of the Native American Church.

Today, Native American religion in the southwest is often a fusion of Indian and Roman Catholic tradition. The Corn Dance is still celebrated alongside Catholic masses. ⑤

45

The Maya, Native Americans who established a powerful civilization in Central America thousands of years ago, built this complex of pyramids and buildings at Kulkulkan. For some reason, the Mayan civilization disappeared around the year A.D. 900, although descendants of the Maya still live in the jungles of Mexico and Central America.

6 Religions of Central and South America

South American Indians are known for their empires. In the years before the Spanish conquest of the 16th century, three empires dominated Central and South America: the Maya, the Aztecs, and the Inca.

Of the three, the Maya was the oldest. This empire lasted for nearly 1,500 years, stretching back to 400 B.C. Mayan land spanned from southern Mexico to Guatemala and Belize. The most distinctive feature of Mayan religion is the pyramid. The pyramids were altars, or bases, for the temples. Their sides were divided into layers, mirroring the Mayan view of the universe.

The Mayan universe had three sections. There was the upper world, where spirits lived. It had 13 layers, each ruled by a different god. Then there was Earth. According to the Maya, there had been three worlds before this one. A flood destroyed each world. Eventually, the Maya believed, a flood will wipe out this world as well. Below the Earth were the nine layers of Xibalba, the Mayan underworld. Xibalba had places of rest and places of suffering. Evil people were punished there. Warriors who died in battle and women who died in childbirth found peace there.

Mayan society was divided into the rulers and the commoners. Shamans worked among the commoners, curing and performing private ceremonies. Priests dealt almost entirely with high-ranking officials. Their ceremonies were part religious, part political. The children of the ruling classes often became priests themselves.

Like the North American Indians, the Maya drew no distinctions between the visible world and the supernatural. All things existed, and everything had a sacred quality. The Mayan word for this was K'ul. For humans and animals, K'ul was found in the blood. Thus, blood was a major part of Mayan rituals.

Mayan gods, known as K'u, could be represented in animal or human form. They had different aspects, depending on gender, color, and direction. The color and direction aspects were linked. For instance, the rain god Chac might be seen as the Black Chac of the West or the Yellow Chac of the South. Blue was a color reserved for sacrifices to the gods.

Offerings to the gods took several different forms. Food and precious metals were often sacrificed. Sometimes animals were sacrificed as well. The most important events, such as the dedication of a temple, required a human sacrifice. Sacrifices were usually prisoners of war. Captives of high rank were sacrificed. Low-ranking captives became slaves. Among modern Maya, blood sacrifices are done using chickens.

Mayans also had a well of sacrifice, dedicated to the rain gods. They threw jade, gold, and incense into the well. Sometimes, humans were thrown in. Anyone who survived the 65-foot drop into the water was questioned. The gods had clearly given him a special message or vision.

Human sacrifice was an important part of the
Aztecs' religion. This drawing from an Aztec
book, called a codex, shows a priest holding the
bleeding heart of a sacrifice victim aloft to the
sun god Huitzilopochtli. Another victim lies at the
foot of the altar. Huitzilopochtli was one of the
most important Aztec gods. The Aztecs believed
that at the end of each night he chased away his
sister, the moon, and his brothers, the stars, so the
new day could begin. Human blood from Aztec
sacrifices was needed to strengthen Huitzilopochtli
on his journey.

AN AZTEC LEGEND

In the first year, a giant monster swam through the darkness. Two gods, Tezcatlipoca and Quetzalcoatl, changed themselves into huge, terrible snakes. They coiled themselves around the monster and squeezed. They squeezed so tightly that the monster split in two. Her back half became the sky; her front half became the Earth. The monster's features changed into the land we know today. Her hair became trees and flowers. Her skin became grass. Her eyes turned into lakes and pools, and her mouth became caves. Her shoulders and elbows became mountains and hills. The monster demanded human hearts to eat. Only then would she grow food to feed the people.

In the last 200 years of the Mayan empire, the Aztecs rose to power in the north. The Aztecs embraced much of the Maya worldview, yet unlike the Mayan K'ul, the Aztec gods' thirst for blood was constant. One of their creation legends makes it clear: Unless the earth was given human hearts, the world would starve.

The Aztec universe was divided into five regions, each with its own gods. Only a few of these gods dealt with humans. Two of them were the ancient enemies Tezcatlipoca and Quetzalcoatl. Tezcatlipoca was the god of night and darkness, while Quetzalcoatl was the feathered serpent of knowledge. Other gods included Tlaloc, the god of rain, and Tonatiuh, the god of the sun. Tonatiuh demanded the bloodiest sacrifices.

Aztec religion, in turn, influenced the Maya. By the time of Spanish conquest, Mayan sacrifice had become more brutal. As in Aztec rituals, the victim would be painted blue and held down. The priest would cut into the victim's chest and remove his heart while it was still beating. He then would smear the blood on a holy *idol*.

In South America at this time, the Incan empire was growing. Incas were fairly tolerant of local religions and allowed conquered tribes to worship their local gods. However, they demanded reverence for the major Incan gods as well.

Like other South American Indians, Incas worshipped the sun god above all others—it was the main active force in their lives. Incas believed the god Viracocha created the universe. Viracocha's children were the sun and the moon. In turn, they gave birth to the morning star and the evening star. These were the grandparents of the human race. The morning star created Lord Earth, who created men. The evening star gave birth to Lady Ocean, the mother of women.

Because of the size of the empire, Inca priests had a complex, ranked organization. The high priest was second only to the emperor in communication with the sun. Below him were 10 priests who supervised others.

Inca sacrifices were generally animals, precious metals, or food. The sacrifice

Unlike Mayas or Aztecs, Incas included women in the priesthood. Priestesses often served in the shrines to the moon.

51

NATIVE AMERICAN LIFE

would also include burning coca leaves, the source of modern cocaine. There were only occasional human sacrifices. Each June, two infants would be buried alive for the Feast of the Sun. September's Feast of the Moon, however, did not require such a sacrifice.

During the early 1500s, the great empires of South America came to an end. The Spanish conquered the Incas, Aztecs, and Maya. The Spanish considered native priests agents of the devil. They were killed or driven into hiding. Many native Mexicans publicly converted to Christianity, the Spaniards' religion, but practiced their own religion privately. The Spanish Inquisition drove many tribes into the Yucatán jungle. Some survive there to this day.

Some Indian tribes were never associated with an empire. The Jivaro Indians of Ecuador are an interesting example. They believe in two gods. There is Nunqui, the Earth Mother, and her husband, Shakema. People only pray to Nunqui.

When Jivaro Indians reach adulthood, they must undergo a

Quetzalcoatl was an important god both for the Aztecs and Maya. This sculpture shows him emerging from the jaws of the earth. Quetzalcoatl is a god of farming and agriculture; Mexican legend has it that he introduced the growth of corn to the people.

maturity ritual. Girls drink a hallucinogenic drink called *natema*. Boys go into the forest alone. There, they hunt and kill a tree sloth. Then they must make a shrunken head, called a *tsantsa*. There is a celebration when they return.

The Jivaro believe that all plants and animals have a soul. People, on the other hand, can have three souls. Everyone gets a soul at birth, called Nekas Wakini. It stays with the body until death, and then remains near the dead person's house. People put out food for the spirit, or else it will turn into a troublesome demon.

Then, there is the Arutam, or the soul for health and safety. This soul must be earned through a vision quest. Having this soul should prevent a person from harm. Only people with Arutam can get the third soul. Muisak is an avenging soul, which lives on after a person dies of foul play. It seeks revenge on whomever is responsible for the victim's death. The only way to stop the Muisak from striking is to shrink the victim's head.

There are two types of Jivaro shamans. Some shamans heal people; others are harmful. Both of them drink natema to contact the spirit world. Jivaro believe that the harmful shamans shoot invisible darts into a person, making them sick or causing them trouble. The healers, on the other hand, ask spirits to remove the invisible darts to make people well. Both men and women can be shamans. Shamans live well, charging high prices to cure or to curse.

When the Spanish came, the Jivaro were one of the few groups who were never conquered. While they have been slightly influenced by missionaries and have limited the practice of head shrinking, they practice the same religion today that they did 200 years ago.

Today, most of the natives of Mexico, Central America, and South America follow the Roman Catholic religion. However, they have incorporated some of the ceremonies and rituals of their ancient religions into their worship services.

The religious life of Native Americans was as colorful as it was diverse. Yet nearly every culture believed in the divinity of all things in nature. Perhaps by understanding this outlook, we can better come to grips with our own place on the planet. S

Chronology

400 B.C. Mayan empire begins.

A.D. 1300 Incas establish capital at Cuzco.

1325 Aztecs found their capital city, Tenochtitlán.

1521 The Spanish capture Tenochtitlán, conquering the Aztecs and bringing the Roman Catholic faith to Mexico.

1524 The Spanish conquer the Mayas and force many to convert to Catholicism.

1532 The Spanish conquer the Incas, again forcing the Native Americans to convert to Christianity.

1760s Delaware Prophet teaches unity and praying only to the Great Spirit.

1763 Ottawa chief Pontiac attacks nine forts; this becomes known as Pontiac's Rebellion.

1766 A peace treaty ends Pontiac's rebellion.

1776 The United States of America declares its independence from England.

1783 The American Revolution ends, and a new country, the United States of America, is established.

1799 Seneca chief Handsome Lake begins to have visions; this leads to the founding of Handsome Lake Church.

1812 War of 1812 begins; most Native Americans side with the British.

1816 Man Chief ends sacrifices of captive Pawnee girls.

1824 Russian Orthodox Church begins missionary work in Alaska.

1830 U.S. government passes the Indian Removal Act.

1838 Cherokees are moved to Oklahoma along the Trail of Tears.

1867 United States buys Alaska.

1869 Transcontinental railroad is completed.

1889 Ghost Dance religion begins.

1890 In December, the Seventh Cavalry kills 200 Sioux men, women, and children at Wounded Knee, South Dakota; John Wilson founds the Big Moon Society; it later adopts many Christian values and becomes the Native American Church.

2003 There are an estimated 3 million Native Americans living in the United States and Canada.

Glossary

animism belief in the existence of spirits separate from bodies.

archaeologist a person who studies material remains of past human life and activities.

convert to change from one religion to another.

diuretic tending to dehydrate the body by increasing sweat and urine flow.

fast to go without food for a period of time.

hallucinogen a substance that causes a person to see or hear things that aren't there.

idol a representation or symbol of an object of worship.

lacrosse a game in which players use a long-handled stick with a mesh pouch for catching, carrying, and throwing a ball at a goal.

longhouse a long dwelling in which several families live.

potlatch a ceremonial feast marked by the host's lavish distribution of gifts with the expectation of eventual reciprocation.

reincarnation rebirth of a soul in a new body.

revere to worship.

scaffold a platform at a height above ground level.

shaman the spiritual leader of a community with powers gained through mystic visions. Also called medicine man.

solstice either of the two points on the ecliptic at which its distance from the celestial equator is greatest and which is reached by the sun each year about June 22nd and December 22nd.

taboo a prohibition against touching, saying, or doing something for fear of immediate harm from a supernatural force.

tinder a flammable substance used as kindling to start a fire.

vision quest a personal, spiritual search undertaken by an adolescent native North American boy in order to learn through a trance or vision.

wampum beads of polished shells strung in strands or belts and used by North American Indians as money and ornaments.

Further Reading

Debelius, Maggie. *The American Indians: The Spirit World.* Alexandria: Time-Life Books, 1992.

Hardin, Terri, ed. *Legends & Lore of the American Indians.* New York: Barnes & Noble Books, 1993.

Meditz, Sandra W., ed. *Islands of the Commonwealth Caribbean.* Washington, D.C.: Library of Congress, 1989.

Moulton, Candy. *Everyday Life among the American Indians.* Cincinnati, Ohio: Writer's Digest Books, 2001.

Milton, Joyce and Robert Orsi, et al. *The Feathered Serpent and the Cross.* London: Cassel, 1980.

Sharer, Robert J. *Daily Life in Maya Civilization.* Westport, Conn.: Greenwood Press, 1996.

Internet Resources

http://www.uwgb.edu/galta/mrr/jivaro/
   This informative site provides a wide range of information on the Jivaro Indians of Ecuador.

http://www.csp.org/communities/docs/fikes-nac_history.html
   The site provides a brief history of the Native American Church.

http://www.heritage.nf.ca/aboriginal/default.html
   This Web site contains information on the aboriginal peoples of Newfoundland and Labrador in Canada.

Index

Picture Credits

3: Hulton/Archive/Getty Images
8: Corbis Images
10: North Wind Picture Archives
12: North Wind Picture Archives
14: Hulton/Archive/Getty Images
17: Hulton/Archive/Getty Images
18: Werner Forman/Art Resource, NY
22: Smithsonian American Art Museum,
     Washington, D.C./Art Resource, NY
27: Smithsonian American Art Museum,
     Washington, D.C./Art Resource, NY
28: The Woolaroc Museum, Bartlesville,
     Oklahoma; (inset) Independence
     National Historical Park, Philadelphia

30: Hulton/Archive/Getty Images
33: Werner Forman/Art Resource, NY
36: Hulton/Archive/Getty Images
38: Geoffrey Clements/Corbis
41: Hulton/Archive/Getty Images
43: Hulton/Archive/Getty Images
44: Hulton/Archive/Getty Images
46: Corbis Images
49: Biblioteca Nazionale, Florence,
     Italy/Art Resource, NY
52: Michael Zabe/Art Resource, NY

Front Cover: Hulton/Archive/Getty Images
Back Cover: North Wind Picture Archives

Contributors

Dr. Troy Johnson is a Professor of American Indian Studies and History at California State University, Long Beach, California. He is an internationally published author and is the author, co-author, or editor of fifteen books, including *Contemporary Political Issues of the American Indian* (1999), *Red Power: The American Indians' Fight for Freedom* (1999), *American Indian Activism: Alcatraz to the Longest Walk* (1997), and *The Occupation of Alcatraz Island: Indian Self-Determination and the Rise of Indian Activism* (1996). He has published numerous scholarly articles, has spoken at conferences across the United States, and is a member of the editorial board of the journals *American Indian Culture and Research* and *The History Teacher.* Dr. Johnson has served as president of the Society of History Education since 2001. He has been profiled in *Reference Encyclopedia of the American Indian* (2000) and *Directory of American Scholars* (2000). He has won awards for his permanent exhibit at Alcatraz Island; he also was named Most Valuable Professor of the Year by California State University, Long Beach, in 1997. He served as associate director and historical consultant on the PBS documentary film *Alcatraz Is Not an Island* (1999), which won first prize at the 26th annual American Indian Film Festival and was screened at the Sundance Film Festival in 2001. Dr. Johnson lives in Long Beach, California.

Rob Staeger lives and writes near Philadelphia. A former newspaper editor, he has written many short stories for young people and several plays for older ones. He has written several nonfiction books, including *Wyatt Earp, The Boom Towns,* and *Native American Sports and Games.*